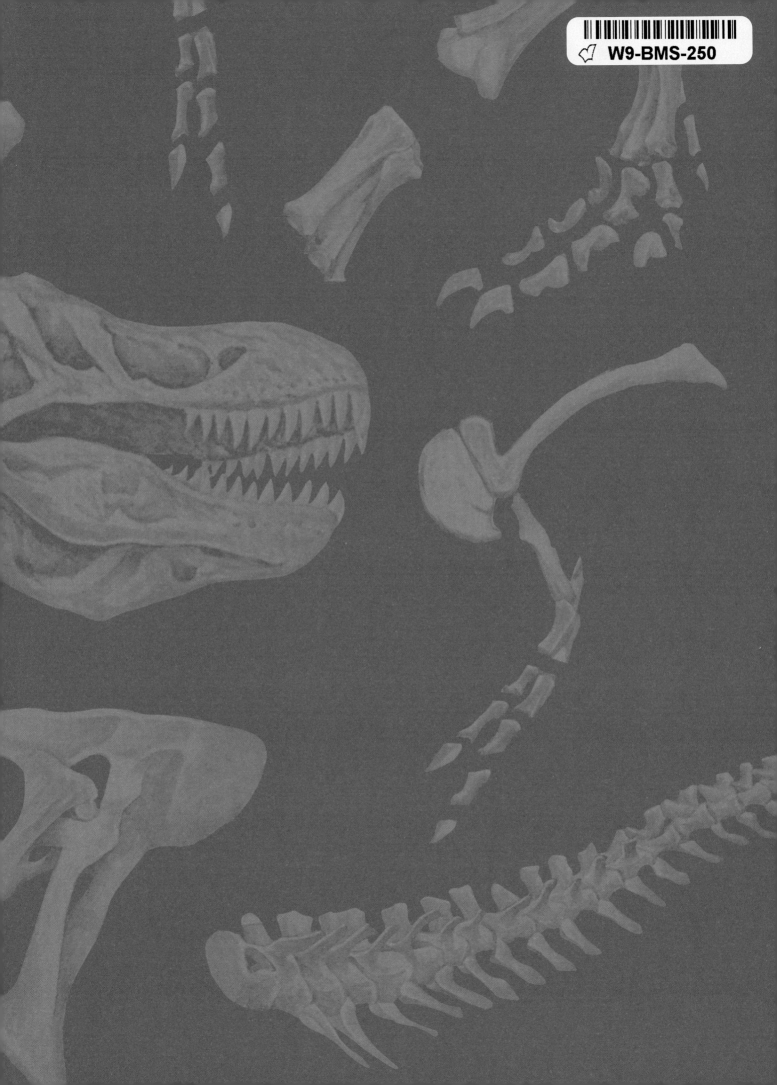

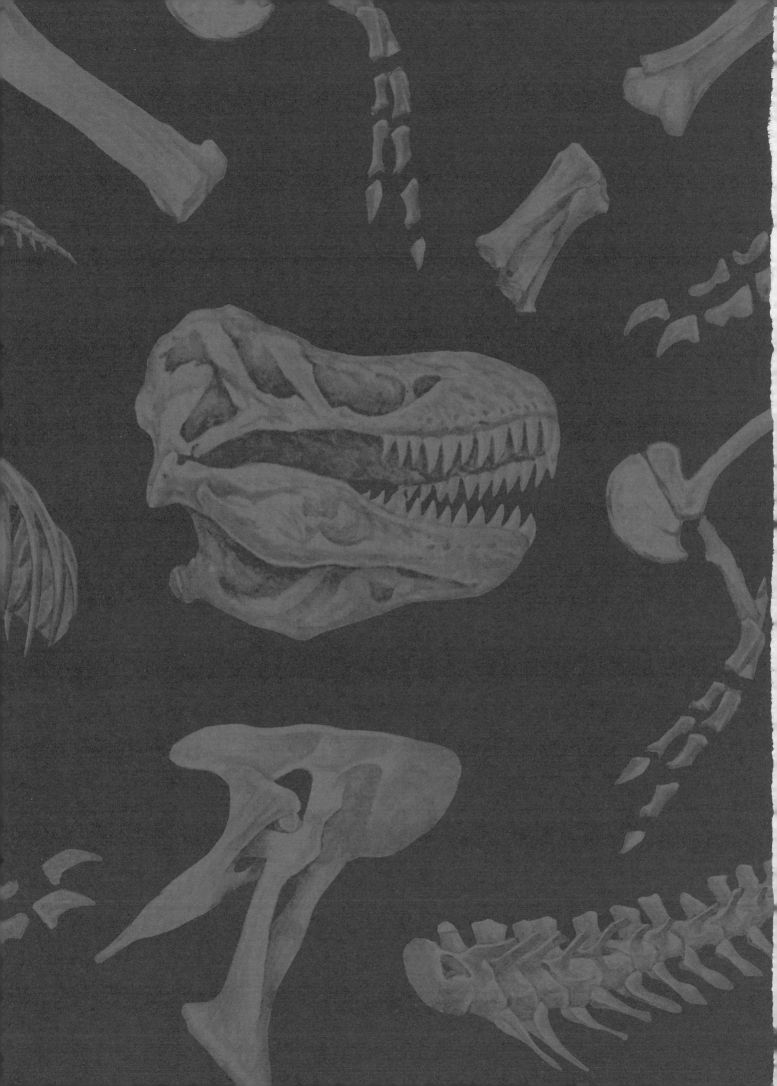

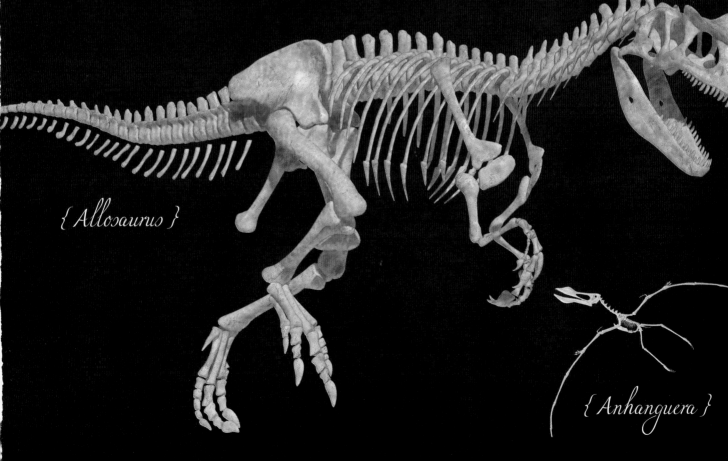

{ Diplodocus }

{ Opthalmosaurus }

{ Pachycephalosaurus }

Bone Collection

DINOSAURS

AND OTHER PREHISTORIC ANIMALS

{ Allosaurus }

{ Anhanguera }

Silver Dolphin Books

An imprint of Printers Row Publishing Group

10350 Barnes Canyon Road, Suite 100, San Diego, CA 92121

www.silverdolphinbooks.com

Copyright © 2017 Quarto Children's Books

Written by Rob Colson
Illustrated by Elizabeth Gray and Steve Kirk
Paper engineering and model illustration by Geoff Rayner/Bag of Badgers Ltd.

Printers Row Publishing Group is a division of Readerlink Distribution Services, LLC. Silver Dolphin Books is a registered trademark of Readerlink Distribution Services, LLC. All notations of errors or omissions should be addressed to Silver Dolphin Books, Editorial Department, at the above address. All other correspondence (author inquiries, permissions) concerning the content of this book should be addressed to Quarto Children's Books Ltd, The Old Brewery, 6 Blundell Street, London N7 9BH UK.

ISBN: 978-1-68412-255-4

Manufactured, printed, and assembled in Shaoguan, China. First printing December 2017.
SL/12/17

PICTURE CREDITS

6cl Nobeastsofierce/Shutterstock, 7t Frans Lanting, Mint images/Science Photo Library, 7c Sinclair Stammers/Science Photo Library, 9t Philcold/Dreamstime, 10bl Ken Lucas, Visuals Unlimited/Science Photo Library, 10-11 Stephen J. Krasemann/Science Photo Library, 13 Dhoxax/ Shutterstock, 14-15 Stocktrek Images, Inc./Alamy, 15cr badztua/Shutterstock, 15b The Natural History Museum/Alamy, 17 Dhoxax/Shutterstock, 18tr Stephen J. Krasemann/Science Photo Library, 18bl Josef Hanus/Shutterstock, 26 Nazzu/Shutterstock, 26-27 Stocktrek Images/Alamy, 30-31 Mark Garlick/Science Photo Library, 31t Animate4.com/Science Photo Library, 31cr Denis Burdin/Shutterstock, 33 Dhoxax/Shutterstock, 35t Dorling Kindersley/Getty, 35b UIG via Getty Images/Getty, 37br Roger Harris/Science Photo Library, 38b Pikoso.kz/Shutterstock, 40-41 Mark Stevenson/Stocktrek Images/Corbis, 41cl Denis Burdin/Shutterstock, 41br Walter Myers/Stocktrek Images/Corbis, 43t Badztua/ Shutterstock, 44-45 Leonello Calvetti/Shutterstock, 45t Leonello Calvetti/Science Photo Library, 46-47 Leonello Calvetti/Shutterstock, 47b Josef Hanus/Shutterstock, 48-49 Leonello Calvetti/Shutterstock, 49 Jorg Hackemann/Shutterstock, 50r blickwinkel/Alamy, 50-51 Natural History Museum, London/Science Photo Library, 52cl Superstock, 52-53 National Geographic Image Collection/Alamy, 53c Pakhnyuschcha/ Shutterstock, 53b Djgis/Shutterstock, 56-57 National Geographic Image Collection/Alamy, 57t Linda Kennedy/Alamy, 57b Shutterstock, 58b Alex Staroseltsev/Shutterstock, 58-59 Lefteris Papaulakis, 61t Alex Staroseltsev/Shutterstock

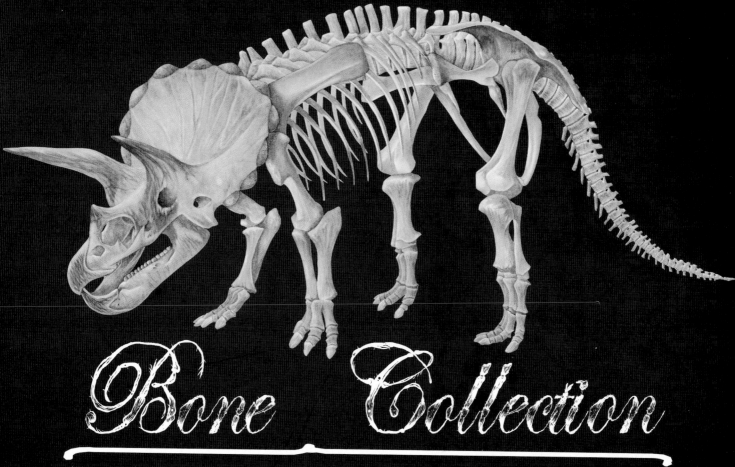

Bone Collection

DINOSAURS

AND OTHER PREHISTORIC ANIMALS

Silver Dolphin

CONTENTS

INTRODUCTION

{ Iguanodon }

FOR 150 million years, life on our planet was dominated by huge **reptiles**. **Dinosaurs** roamed the land, while **pterosaurs** ruled the skies, and **plesiosaurs** and **ichthyosaurs** patrolled the oceans.

{ Kronosaurus }

Then, about 66 million years ago, these prehistoric creatures disappeared, unable to cope with a sudden change in the climate. Other animals, such as birds and **mammals**, survived and took their place. We know about prehistoric animals from the remains they left behind as **fossils**. Today, new fossils are being discovered all the time, changing how we think about these remarkable creatures. Using fossils, scientists work out what the animals looked like and how they lived. Take a look at the bones of dinosaurs and other prehistoric animals, and discover how these creatures looked and lived millions of years ago.

{ Ankylosaurus }

LIFE BEFORE THE DINOSAURS

LIFE on Earth began over 3.5 billion years ago. The first life forms were tiny single-celled microbes that lived in the warm oceans. For nearly three billion years this was the only life on Earth. Then, about 600 million years ago, multicelled life forms appeared, including the first animals.

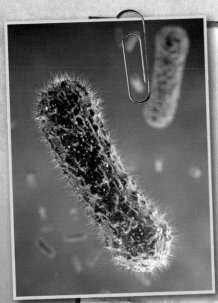

Bacteria

Single-celled bacteria are simple life forms, measuring less than one thousandth of an inch long. Bacteria were among the first life to appear on Earth and are still the most common life form on the planet today.

EARLY FISH

The first fishlike creatures appeared about 500 million years ago. They were jawless and toothless fish known as agnathans.

Endoceras

Strictoporella

Sacabambaspis

Triarthrus

Coral

CAMBRIAN EXPLOSION

Many kinds of life appeared on Earth during an 80-million-year period that began 541 million years ago, called the **Cambrian** Explosion. The seas teemed with a huge number and variety of animals.

GIANT SEA HUNTERS

Sea scorpions first appeared in the oceans 400 million years ago. These **predators** could grow up to six feet long.

{ Fossil of a trilobite }

∽◈ TRILOBITE ◈∽

Trilobites were seabed-dwelling creatures that became common in oceans all over the world early in the Cambrian Explosion. With their tough external shells and jointed limbs, trilobites were distant relatives of today's crabs and lobsters. More than 17,000 **species** of trilobites have been identified.

Nautiloids

A scene from Ordovician times around 450 million years ago.

Cyclonema

Promissum

Strophomena

Rugose corals

TIMELINE

BELOW we trace the development of life over the last 250 million years. During this time, the face of the planet has changed dramatically, as one giant continent, known as **Pangaea**, split up to form the continents and oceans we know today.

TRIASSIC
252–201 m.y.a.

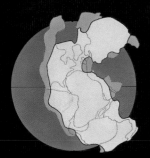

Pangaea began to break up. The first dinosaurs and pterosaurs started to appear.

m.y.a. = million years ago

JURASSIC
201–145 m.y.a.

As new continents formed, deserts became rain forests. Giant dinosaurs dominated the land and the first birds appeared.

SYNAPSIDS

Shonisaurus

Eurhinosaurus

Plesiosaurus

CROCODYLOMORPHS

Dimorphodon

Stegosaurus

Allosaurus

Saltopus

Archaeopteryx

MASS EXTINCTION

The dinosaurs and many other large animals became **extinct** 66 million years ago. A **meteorite** collided with Earth, causing a sudden cooling of the climate.

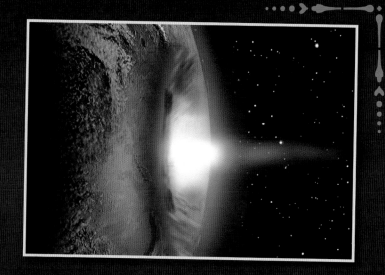

CRETACEOUS	CENOZOIC
145-66 m.y.a.	66 m.y.a.-present day

Today's continents started taking shape. Flowering plants and placental mammals appeared.

Following a meteorite strike, the climate cooled. The giant reptiles disappeared, and smaller mammals and birds dominated in their place.

TORTOISES/TURTLES

MAMMALS

Nimravus

ICHTHYOSAURS

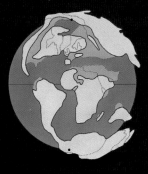

PLESIOSAURS

Kronosaurus

Woolly Mammoth

LIZARDS

SNAKES

TRUE CROCODILES

PTEROSAURS

Pteranodon

ORNITHISCHIA

Iguanodon

THEROPODA

BIRDS

Tyrannosaurus

Neocathartes

9

EARLY
LAND ANIMALS

ABOUT 330 million years ago, forests extended over most low-lying tropical landscapes. Among the many kinds of four-legged **vertebrates** living in the forests were early **amphibians** and reptile-like animals. The wooded areas were also home to giant eurypterids and insects.

THE COAL AGE

This time of large forests is known as the **Carboniferous** period, which means "coal-making." Remains of the trees in the giant forests of this time became layers of coal in the ground.

Legs of *Dimetrodon* splayed out to the sides of its body, like those of a modern reptile.

⤜ EARLY AMPHIBIAN ⤛

This fossil of an early amphibian was found in North America. Amphibians evolved from fish that had simple lungs for breathing air. The first amphibians still spent a lot of time in the water and, like amphibians today, they had to return to water to breed.

{ Early amphibian fossil from Carboniferous period, found in Ohio }

PERMIAN TIMES

By 250 million years ago, during a period called the **Permian**, the land was dominated by reptiles and the ancestors of mammals. Some of them grew to nearly 17 feet long. At this time, the largest dinosaurs had not yet appeared.

Sharp teeth

Rib cage protected the vital organs in a narrow body.

Dimetrodon's sail back helped it to warm up in the morning sun.

In Permian times, hunters such as *Lycaenops* (right) preyed on plant-eaters such as *Robertia* (left) and *Dicynodon* (center).

BREEDING ON LAND

Unlike amphibians, early land animals called **synapsids** could lay their eggs on land. The synapsids, such as the meat-eating *Dimetrodon* (left), are the ancestors of mammals.

SMALL PREDATORS

SOME of the smallest dinosaurs were fast-moving, two-legged predators. The smallest dinosaurs of all, such as *Saltopus*, were about the size of a chicken, weighing as little as two pounds.

Feathered Body

The birdlike *Protarchaeopteryx* had feathers, but probably could not fly. Its chest, tail, and upper legs were covered with downy feathers one inch long. Clusters of long feathers grew on its arms and at the end of its tail.

PREY
These small predators had a varied diet, including lizards, frogs, small mammals, and insects.

Short arms

TURKEY-SIZED DINOSAUR

Compsognathus (right) was a two-legged predator that was built for speed. Like modern birds, it had hollow bones, which made it lighter. It also had a long neck and tail, and long shins suitable for fast running. Its short hands had three pincerlike fingers for grabbing **prey**.

Strong claws on both hands

{ Skull }

SKULL

Compsognathus had a long, narrow skull, with large sockets for its eyes. It had sharp eyesight for spotting fast-moving prey.

DINO MYSTERY

Very little is known about *Saltopus* because very few pieces of its skeleton have been found.

Small, sharp teeth

WHOLE FOSSILS

Compsognathus lived 150 million years ago, and lived near lagoons on wooded islands. Two well-preserved fossils of *Compsognathus* have been found. We know what they ate because the remains of lizards were found in the stomachs of both fossils.

{ Complete fossil }

ORNITHOLESTES

A swift hunter, *Ornitholestes* lived about 150 million years ago in North America. This dinosaur weighed about as much as a small dog. It may have used its excellent eyesight to hunt at night.

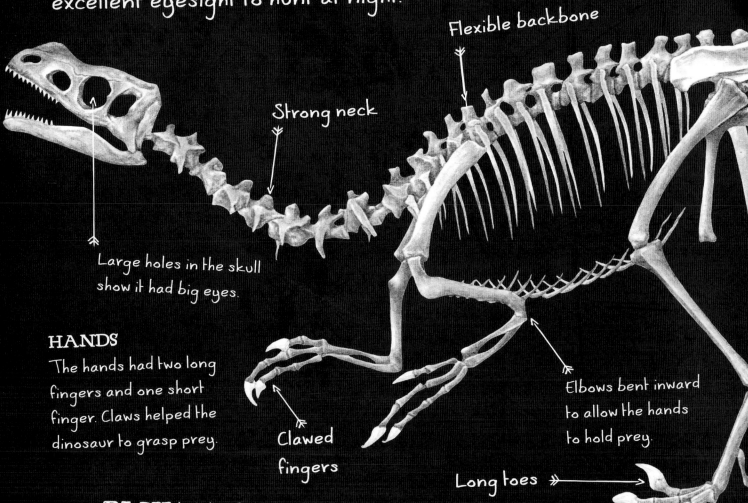

Flexible backbone

Strong neck

Large holes in the skull show it had big eyes.

HANDS
The hands had two long fingers and one short finger. Claws helped the dinosaur to grasp prey.

Clawed fingers

Elbows bent inward to allow the hands to hold prey.

Long toes ➤

BUILT TO HUNT
Ornitholestes had many features that helped it catch small prey. It was fast and agile and ran on two legs. It could use its arms to hold onto prey and had sharp teeth and a strong jaw to bite into flesh. It had large eyes that gave it excellent vision, even in dim light.

TAIL

The long tail made up more than half the dinosaur's body length.

Tail was held high as it ran.

POSSIBLE PACK HUNTER

Some scientists think that *Ornitholestes* may have been a pack hunter. With its strong jaw and sharp, cone-shaped teeth, it could have joined others to bring down larger prey such as young *Camptosaurus*.

LEGS

The bones in the back legs were light, and the toe bones were long and slender. This was perfect for running quickly.

Sharp claws

Misnamed

The name Ornitholestes means "bird robber." The dinosaur was once thought to have hunted birds, but we now know that it probably preyed on lizards as there were few birds around at the time.

Ornitholestes was about six feet long and weighed 25 pounds.

GALLIMIMUS

Ribs

Hipbone

Tail vertebrae

THE fast-running *Gallimimus* was an ornithomimid, or "bird mimic" dinosaur. This lightweight **theropod** probably moved across open plains in groups, searching for food. It had a small head and a toothless jaw with a beak for cutting plant food.

Pelvis

Long, lightweight legs »

BUILT FOR SPEED

Gallimimus had long legs and short toes that were ideal for running. It held its tail out straight as it ran to stay balanced. Its arms may have been covered in downy feathers.

Short toes »

RUNNING AWAY

Gallimimus had to watch out for predators such as the tyrannosaurid *Tarbosaurus*. Its best defense was its ability to run away.

Large eye sockets

Shoulder

Neck vertebrae

Toothless mouth

Long, flexible neck supported a small, lightweight head.

BIG EYES

Like ostriches, *Gallimimus* had large eyes, which were placed on the sides of its head, allowing it to spot danger from far away.

SLENDER HANDS

Gallimimus's hands had three clawed fingers, which it could use to pull down the branches of trees to reach the plant foliage.

Claws on each finger

Gallimimus was about 15 feet long—twice the length of an ostrich.

Varied Diet

Gallimimus lived in eastern Asia around 70 million years ago. It may have fed on tender water plants, but may also have eaten small animals.

17

DROMAEOSAURUS

A small but fierce hunter, *Dromaeosaurus* was well armed, with a long, hooked claw on the second toe of each foot, sharp teeth, and a strong bite. It lived in North America about 70 million years ago.

Dromaeosaurus walked on two legs.

Strong muscles in the tail helped to keep it stiff.

Sickle Claws

When hunting, *Dromaeosaurus* leapt off the ground to pounce on its prey. It tore at the flesh with the claws on its feet, which were hooked like the blades of a sickle.

STIFF TAIL

The long tail provided balance as the dinosaur ran, just like the tail of a cheetah does today. The dinosaur could sprint at up to 40 mph.

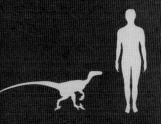

Dromaeosaurus was about six feet long from nose to tail.

GUESSWORK

A complete skeleton has never been found, so we do not know its exact body shape. Some scientists believe that its body may have been covered in brightly colored feathers.

Birdlike hipbone

Large eye socket

The large head had powerful jaw muscles.

Teeth

TEETH

The teeth curved backward. This allowed the dinosaur to keep a tight grip on its prey.

Hands had three long fingers with hooked claws.

Long leg bones

PACK HUNTER

Dromaeosaurus hunted in packs. A large pack could bring down prey that was much bigger than any of the individual hunters. These hunters had large brains, which they used to help them work together during a hunt.

As it ran, it held its sickle claws off the ground.

IGUANODONTS

THE iguanodonts were heavy plant-eaters that moved around slowly, browsing on shrubs and trees. Iguanodonts reached their peak success around 110 million years ago, when they lived all around the world.

A tall fin on the back may have supported strong muscles.

OUT OF DATE?

Iguanodonts were one of the first groups of dinosaurs to be found and one of the best known groups of plant-eating dinosaurs. Widespread fossil remains were discovered from Mid **Jurassic** to Late **Cretaceous** times. However, modern research does not generally recognize the group and the name is only used informally.

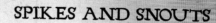

SPIKES AND SNOUTS

Probactrosaurus was a plant-eating dinosaur that combined features of iguanodonts and hadrosaurs. It had five-fingered hands, which are typical of iguanodonts, as well as a wide, flat snout.

Sarcosuchus, an ancient relative of the crocodile, lived alongside Ouranosaurus.

Probactrosaurus was 18 feet long and weighed a little more than one ton.

SENSE OF SMELL

Muttaburrasaurus is one of the few dinosaur fossils to have been discovered in Australia. It was similar in appearance to *Iguanodon* but had larger nostrils. It probably relied on its keen sense of smell to find food.

Ouranosaurus drinking at a watering hole.

SAIL BACK

Ouranosaurus had a tall, sail-like ridge on its back, similar to that seen on the meat-eating Spinosaurus. Like iguanodonts, Ouranosaurus also had thumb spikes.

21

IGUANODON

WHEN an *Iguanodon* shin bone was discovered in England in 1809, it was believed to have belonged to a giant mammal. Later discoveries confirmed that it was a dinosaur.

THUMB SPIKE

Iguanodon had a sharp spike on each thumb, which it used to defend itself.

Thumb spike

Five-fingered hands

Iguanodon could walk on four legs or two.

STRONG LEGS

To support the *Iguanodon's* weight, the leg bones were thick and strong.

Hooflike nails

Iguanodon was 30 feet long and weighed five tons.

BROWSING HERDS

Herds of *Iguanodons* were common across Europe between 128 and 110 million years ago.

Bony tendons crisscrossed the backbone, giving it extra strength.

The tail muscles attached to these spikes and extensions above and below the bones in the tail.

Heavy tail was held straight when the dinosaur walked on two legs.

EXTENSIVE REMAINS

Many nearly complete skeletons of *Iguanodons* have been discovered, which makes this one of the best-understood dinosaurs. The largest find was made in 1878, when the remains of 38 *Iguanodon* were found in a Belgian coal mine.

V-shaped bones gave the tail extra protection.

← ← Pelvis bone

FOOTPRINTS

Footprints of *Iguanodon* have been discovered in rocks in southern England. These show the animals walking on two legs and traveling in a herd.

LAMBEOSAURUS

THE sturdily built *Lambeosaurus* belonged to a group of plant-eaters called hadrosaurs, also known as duck-bills. It used its toothless, horn-covered beak to nip leaves from the ends of plants. *Lambeosaurus* lived in North America about 76 million years ago.

EASY BROWSER

Lambeosaurus moved around on all fours, browsing on low-growing plants. It had a flexible neck with strong muscles, which allowed it to gather food around a wide area without having to move its heavy body too much.

Hollow crest may have been used in courtship display or to make loud calls like a horn.

Flat beak was protected by hard horn.

Front legs

Lambeosaurus was 30 feet long and weighed about three tons.

Birdlike pelvis

Attachment points for tail muscles

Heavy tail

GRINDING TEETH

Lambeosaurus had rows of teeth at the back of its mouth to grind up its tough plant food. The teeth would wear out and were replaced with new ones throughout the dinosaur's life.

CROUCHING

This skeleton shows *Lambeosaurus* on all fours. It could also rear up on two legs to run away from predators.

Thick leg bones

Bony spike pointed backward from crest.

Hooflike nails on the toes for walking.

PLATED DINOSAURS

PLATED dinosaurs such as stegosaurs were plant-eaters with small heads and massive bodies. With their heavy armor to protect them, they usually stood their ground against theropod predators such as *Yangchuanosaurus*.

SMALL HEAD

Tuojiangosaurus had a skull that was just 15 inches long that protected a tiny brain.

TAIL ATTACK

The stegosaurs were slow-moving and had brains the size of a walnut. They could not run to escape danger, but would swipe at predators with their powerful tails.

← Tail spikes

SCELIDOSAURUS

Scelidosaurus lived about 190 million years ago and may have been part of an ancestral group of both the stegosaurs and ankylosaurs. The plates on its back were studded with parallel rows of backward-facing spikes. It used its toothless beak to tear at leaves.

{ *Scelidosaurus* fossils have been discovered in Dorset, England }

JURASSIC DINOSAUR

The stegosaurs first appeared about 170 million years ago.
However, by 140 million years ago, most of them had disappeared.
Along with most of the giant sauropods, they died
out at the end of the Jurassic period.

Yangchuanosaurus
hunting prey.

Large
shoulder
spines

GIGANTSPINOSAURUS
This medium-sized stegosaur lived in China
160 million years ago. It is named after the
two huge spines on its shoulders.

STEGOSAURUS

THE slow-moving *Stegosaurus* was the largest member of the group of plant-eating stegosaurs. It had a small head and a huge body topped with two rows of bony plates. This well-protected dinosaur defended itself with its spike-tipped tail.

Stegosaurus was more than 20 feet long.

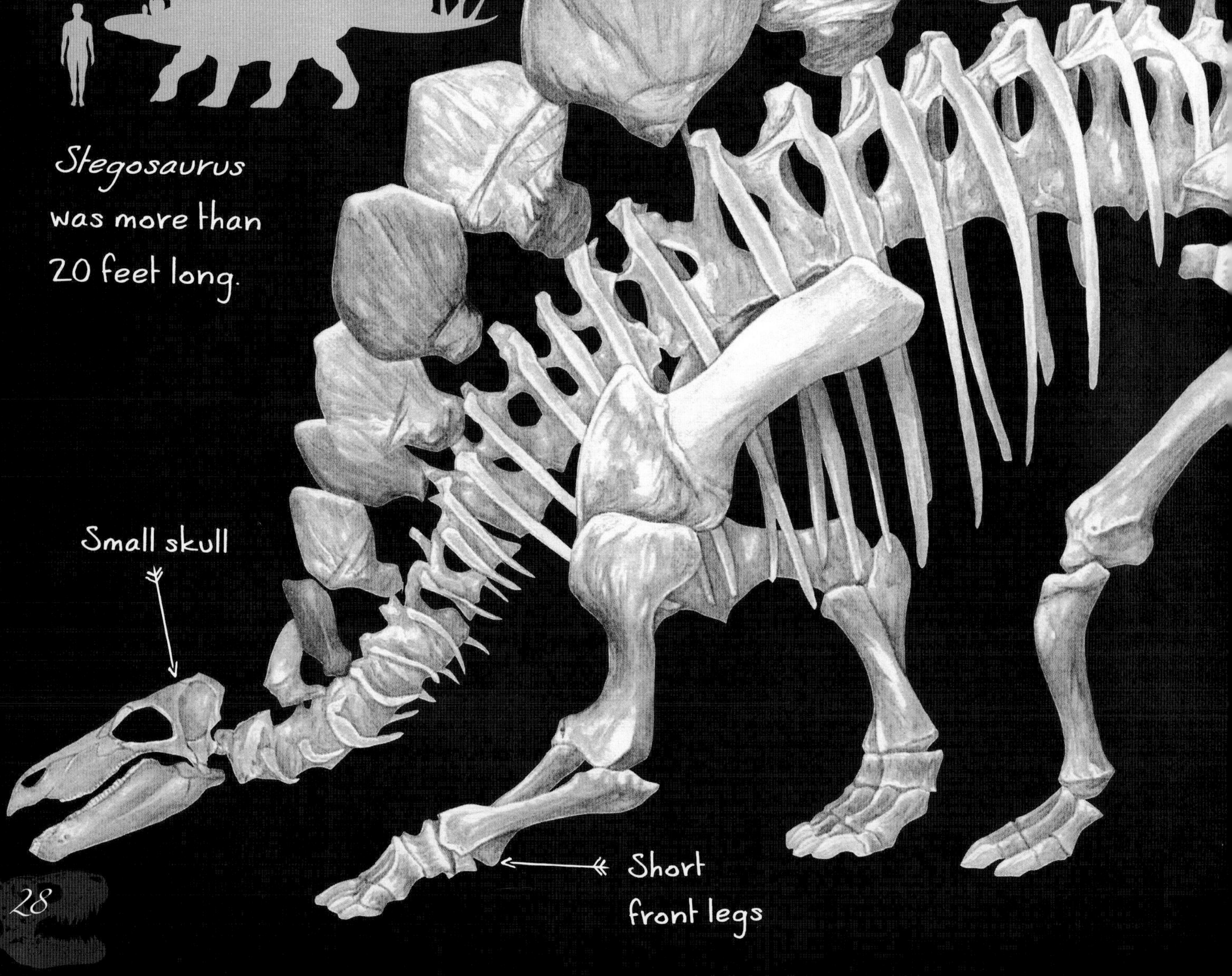

Small skull

Short front legs

BUILD YOUR OWN
STEGOSAURUS
SKELETON AT THE
END OF THE BOOK!

REACHING LEAVES

Stegosaurus lived in North America about 150 million years ago. It could reach the leaves of tree ferns by rearing up on two legs.

Flattened, bony plates

TEMPERATURE CONTROL

The bony plates were covered in blood-rich skin. When the dinosaur was cold, it would turn its side to the sun to warm up. When hot, it would face away from the sun and release heat through the plates.

Broad pelvis

STRONG LEGS

Stegosaurus's massive back legs were more than twice as long as its front legs. This allowed it to reach low-growing plants to eat.

Powerful muscles swung the spiked tail from side to side.

29

TYRANNOSAURS

THE tyrannosaurs were huge, two-legged hunters that lived in North America and Asia more than 66 million years ago, during the Late Cretaceous Period.

Tail held out to balance the dinosaur during a chase.

ON THE HUNT

Dinosaur experts have argued about whether tyrannosaurs were hunters or if they simply fed off the dead bodies of other animals. Research suggests that, because of their acute sense of smell, the tyrannosaurs were primarily **scavengers**, but also hunters when necessary.

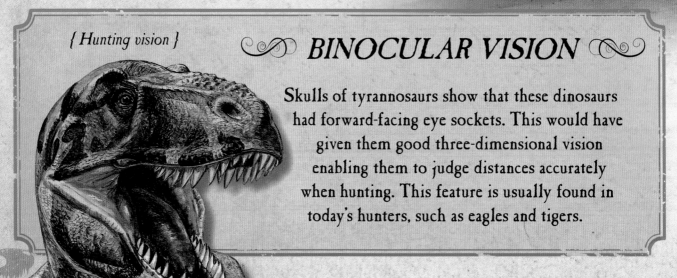

{ Hunting vision }

᭡᭡ BINOCULAR VISION ᭡᭡

Skulls of tyrannosaurs show that these dinosaurs had forward-facing eye sockets. This would have given them good three-dimensional vision enabling them to judge distances accurately when hunting. This feature is usually found in today's hunters, such as eagles and tigers.

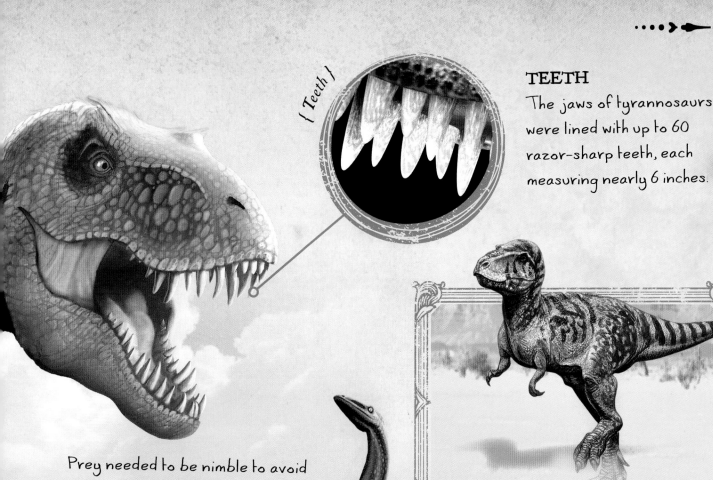

TEETH
The jaws of tyrannosaurs were lined with up to 60 razor-sharp teeth, each measuring nearly 6 inches.

{ Teeth }

Prey needed to be nimble to avoid a tyrannosaur's huge jaws.

SIAMOTYRANNUS
This tyrannosaurlike dinosaur lived in what is now Southeast Asia and grew to 23 feet long. It may have hunted plant-eaters that were much bigger than it was.

MUSCLES
Tyrannosaurs had powerful necks and jaw muscles that allowed them to deliver a bite with great and crippling force.

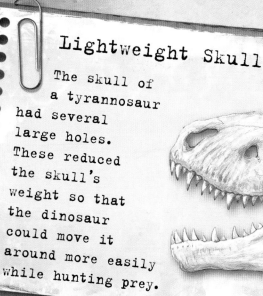

Lightweight Skull
The skull of a tyrannosaur had several large holes. These reduced the skull's weight so that the dinosaur could move it around more easily while hunting prey.

31

TYRANNOSAURUS

MASSIVE and ferocious, *Tyrannosaurus* was a tyrannosaur—a group of meat-eating dinosaurs of the Jurassic and Cretaceous periods. Early tyrannosaurs were small, but later ones were bulky animals with powerful jaws and sharp teeth. *Tyrannosaurus* was one of the largest, and fiercest.

LIGHTWEIGHT

Its skeleton was big enough to support the hunter's vast bulk, but also light enough to allow it to move quickly to catch prey.

Tail vertebrae

Thigh bone

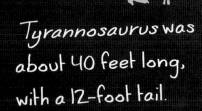

Tyrannosaurus was about 40 feet long, with a 12-foot tail.

TAIL BALANCE

Like other dinosaurs that walked on two legs, *Tyrannosaurus* held its long tail straight out behind it. This helped balance the weight of the front part of its body, including its massive head.

TYRANNOSAURUS REX

Neck vertebrae

Shoulder blade →

BIG HEAD

The massive skull was nearly four feet long, and its monstrous jaws and teeth could rip prey apart in seconds.

Razor-sharp teeth

SHORT ARMS

Tyrannosaurus had surprisingly short arms compared to the rest of its huge body.

Special ribs lined the dinosaur's belly to help strengthen this part of its body.

Two claws on each arm

Lizard Ruler

This giant hunter lived in North America some 68 to 66 million years ago, during the Late Cretaceous Period. Translated from Greek, its name means "tyrant lizard."

GIGANOTOSAURUS

A huge creature that lived 100 million years ago in South America, *Giganotosaurus* was a fearsome predator. Weighing 8 tons, these meat-eaters had big appetites, and they may have hunted in packs to take down giant sauropods such as *Argentinosaurus*.

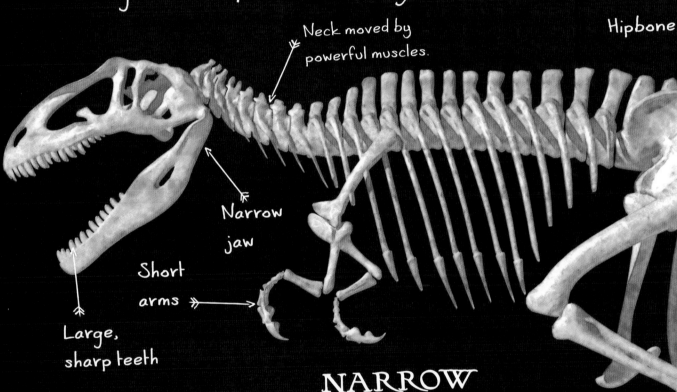

Neck moved by powerful muscles.

Hipbone

Narrow jaw

Short arms

Large, sharp teeth

Giganotosaurus was 44 feet long from head to tail.

NARROW SKULL

Although it was bigger than *Tyrannosaurus rex*, *Giganotosaurus*'s bite was only one-third as powerful. Its narrow skull and lower jaws were adapted to inflict slicing wounds on prey.

Strong feet

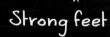

CLAWED FINGERS

Giganotosaurus had short but powerful arms. Each hand was armed with three-clawed fingers.

SHORT SPRINTS

Giganotosaurus walked on two legs and could probably sprint at speeds of up to 20 mph.

SMALL BRAIN

Inside its narrow head, *Giganotosaurus* had a relatively small brain, which was probably the size and shape of a banana.

Long tail

Giganotosaurus's huge body meant that this massive dinosaur weighed up to 14 tons, about the weight of three elephants.

Bones in the tail

Ankle

Sharp Tooth

Giganotosaurus's teeth were up to 8 inches long. The teeth were constantly replaced as they wore out. The U-shaped groove at the root of the tooth shows where a replacement tooth was growing.

ALLOSAURUS

THE theropod *Allosaurus* lived 150 million years ago. This dinosaur was the largest meat-eater of its time. It may have hunted on its own or worked in packs to bring down large prey such as the giant *Apatosaurus*.

Large, heavy hipbone

AMBUSH HUNTER

Allosaurus preyed on the dozens of species of plant-eaters that lived on the open plains. It was an **ambush hunter** that would lie and wait for prey such as *Camptosaurus*, and pounce on any that strayed too close.

The legs were relatively short, meaning that *Allosaurus* was not a very fast runner.

Allosaurus may have grown to 40 feet long and weighed up to 2.5 tons.

Hooflike claws on feet

SHORT SPRINTS

This predator was too big and heavy to run for long, so it had to catch its prey in short sprints.

Thick neck ↘

FLEXIBLE JOINTS

The skull bones were joined together loosely, making the skull flexible and strong.

Brow ridges ↓

Lower jaw ↗

Teeth had sawlike ↘ edges on both sides.

LIGHT SKULL

Allosaurus's massive head was nearly three feet long. Openings, or windows, between the skull bones made the head much lighter.

Broad rib cage

Three-clawed ↠→ hand

HORNED FOREHEAD

Horned bumps above the eyes may have been used for display or as weapons in battles with other Allosauruses.

PSITTACOSAURUS

WITH a rounded skull and toothless, curved beak, *Psittacosaurus*'s name means "parrot lizard." It was a plant-eater and used its strong beak to break off tough leaves and stems.

The beak was also suited for cracking nuts.

↗ Flexible neck

Short arms ↘

BLUNT CLAWS
The dinosaur had four blunt claws on each hand. ↘

HORNED CHEEKS

Psittacosaurus's cheek bones bulged outward into horned projections. These would develop into spikes as it evolved.

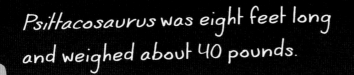

Psittacosaurus was eight feet long and weighed about 40 pounds.

FOUND FOSSILS

More than 400 fossils of *Psittacosaurus* have been found, including several complete skeletons. This is one of the dinosaurs that scientists know the most about.

↗ Birdlike pelvis

← Rib cage

← ← Elbow

HERDING YOUNG

Young *Psittacosaurus* banded together in herds for protection.

Toe bones ↘

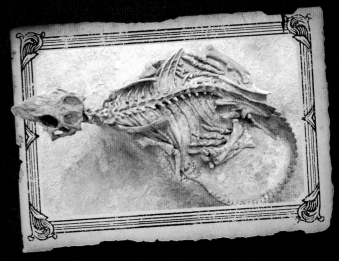

HATCHLING

This fossil of a young *Psittacosaurus* was found in Mongolia. Its body is five inches long. It died soon after hatching.

FRILLED DINOSAURS

PLANT-EATING, frilled ceratopsids such as *Triceratops* were a common sight in the Late Cretaceous Period between 100 and 66 million years ago.

DEFENSE

All ceratopsids were armed with broad neck frills and long, pointed horns. These were found on their enormous heads, which could measure up to eight feet long.

The frill protected the neck from a predator's downward bite.

PROTECTIVE RING

Some studies suggest that ceratopsids worked together when threatened to create a defensive ring of horns.

SPIKED FRILL

Styracosaurus was well-equipped to fight off an attacking tyrannosaur. The enormous frill, with six large spikes growing out from it, protected its neck. It would also use its long nose spike to rip into the flesh of a predator.

{ *Styracosaurus* }

BATTLING HORNS

Horns were not just for defense. Male horned dinosaurs may have used them to battle each other for leadership of the herd. Rivals locked horns and pushed against one another with their neck frills.

MONTANOCERATOPS

The leptoceratopsid *Montanoceratops* had a deep, flexible tail, which may have been waved as a courtship signal. Unlike the more advanced ceratopsids, it had claws on its feet instead of hooves.

Plant-Eater

Once a horned dinosaur had snipped off a plant using its beak, it used large teeth in each cheek to chew the food before swallowing it.

TRICERATOPS

LONG, sharp horns and a bony frill around its neck kept *Triceratops* safe from the fiercest of enemies. *Triceratops* was a heavy plant-eater that browsed on rich, low-growing vegetation.

Backbone had extra vertebrae to strengthen the body.

Triceratops was 30 feet long, 10 feet tall, and weighed more than nine tons.

Rib cage

Short, thick tail

With its heavy body and legs, *Triceratops* had a top speed of 10 mph.

THICK LEGS
The thick legs on this dinosaur were strong enough to carry the weight of the creature's huge body and head.

Short, wide toes

DAGGERS

If threatened by a predator, *Triceratops* would charge, just like a rhinoceros, and use its horns as huge daggers to fight off the attacker.

Neck frill

THREE HORNS

Triceratops's name means "three-horned face." It had two horns on its brow that were up to three feet long. It also had a smaller horn on its nose.

‹ Brow horn

‹ Nose horn

Grinding teeth

Shorter front legs

BEAK

Triceratops had a beak at the front of its mouth that it used to snip off plant material.

‹ Beak

ANKYLOSAURUS

BUILT like a tank, the heavily armored *Ankylosaurus* was a formidable opponent to any potential predator. It had thick skin that was covered with bony plates and had a powerful tail club. This slow-moving plant-eater lived 66 million years ago in North America.

Ankylosaurus was 30 feet long and weighed about four tons.

Hipbones fused to vertebrae

Head spikes

Thick neck

Large nasal cavities inside skull

Broad rib cage

HEAD SPIKES

Ankylosaurus had a broad head with a blunt snout. A pair of spikes grew out of the back of its head, and another pair grew from its cheeks.

FUSED HIPS

To give their bodies extra strength, the massive hipbones were fused to eight of the vertebrae in the backbone.

Hooflike claws

Lying Low

The only way a predator could harm a fully grown Ankylosaurus was to attack its soft belly. But not even a tyrannosaur could tip one over if it crouched down.

SENSE OF SMELL

Ankylosaurus had large nasal cavities inside its skull, giving it a keen sense of smell so that it could sniff out its food.

TAIL DEFENSE

Ankyolsaurus could break the bones of an attacker with its tail club, which it would swing sideways. The bones in the tail were connected to one another by thick tendons, making the tail stiff and very strong.

Strong, short legs

Strong tail

Tail club

NO RUSH

Its huge weight and short legs made Ankylosaurus one of the slowest dinosaurs of all. It probably had a top speed of about 6 mph.

SLOW-WITTED

With a defensive strategy that involved staying still, Ankylosaurus did not need to do a lot of thinking. Its brain was almost as small as that of Stegosaurus.

PACHYCEPHALOSAURUS

'THE name *Pachycephalosaurus* means "thick-headed lizard" and the distinctive domed head of this creature was probably used by males when fighting each other. This was the last of the pachycephalosaurs to become extinct.

RUNNING HERD

Pachycephalosaurus lived in small herds in coastal areas. The whole herd ran away when threatened by a predator. They walked upright on two legs. When running, the dinosaurs held their tails straight to stay balanced.

Upper leg bone

Heavy, rigid tail

Pachycephalosaurus grew to 15 feet long and weighed up to 1,000 pounds.

GOATLIKE LIFESTYLE

Pachycephalosaurs may have had a similar lifestyle to that of mountain goats today. However, there is little fossil evidence to support the idea that they lived in mountainous regions.

Broad feet

SOLID BONE

The *Pachycephalosaurus* skull was made of solid bone 10 inches thick. This protected its small brain like a crash helmet.

The back was held horizontally while running.

Skull was covered in small knobs.

The neck was short and thick.

Pointed beak

SKULL REMAINS

Pachycephalosaurus lived in North America. Parts of its skeleton have been found. Its head was two feet long, making it the largest of the pachycephalosaurs.

Knee

Five-fingered hands

PLANT-EATER

Standing tall on two legs helped the dinosaur to reach vegetation on low tree branches. It had short, sharp teeth that were perfect for shredding leaves and stems.

DIPLODOCUS

THE slow-moving Diplodocus was one of the longest animals to walk on Earth. Only very large predators such as *Allosaurus* posed a threat to these sauropods, which lived in herds of small family groups, as elephants do today.

Small head

HIGH NOSTRILS

The nostrils were right at the top of the head. This led some scientists to believe that *Diplodocus* lived in water, breathing with its head mostly submerged. Now, scientists think that the nostrils were there to keep them out of the way of twigs as the dinosaur ate.

The neck was 20 feet long.

Diplodocus's vertebrae were partly hollow, which made the dinosaur much lighter.

BIG HEART

To provide enough power to pump blood all the way along its neck to the head, *Diplodocus* needed a big heart. Its heart may have weighed as much as a ton.

Diplodocus was more than 100 feet long and weighed about 10 tons.

Diplodocus walked on the tips of its toes.

Shoulder blade

The hipbones were fused to the vertebrae to give extra strength.

Leaf-Stripper

Diplodocus lived in North America about 140 million years ago. It fed on plants, stripping leaves from trees with its rows of small teeth.

LONG TAIL
The tail was made from more than 70 vertebrae. Diplodocus carried its tail off the ground as it walked.

Bones at the end of the tail were very thin.

The heavy body was supported on pillarlike legs.

TAIL WHIP
Marks on the bones in the tail show that they were attached to powerful muscles. Diplodocus would use the tail like a whip, lashing it from side to side to fend off attackers.

The first toe on each foot had a large claw.

ARCHAEOPTERYX

THE earliest known bird, *Archaeopteryx*, lived in Europe about 150 million years ago. Like dinosaurs, *Archaeopteryx* had a long, bony tail. The tail was fringed by feathers, which would have helped it to glide through the air.

GLIDER

Archaeopteryx lacked the large breastbone of modern birds, which means that it could only flap its wings weakly. It relied mainly on gliding.

Tail

Long tail was covered in feathers.

TREE CLIMBER

Archaeopteryx was not a strong flier. It would climb trees using its claws and launch itself from a great height. It would then soar through the air in search of prey.

Long, thin leg bones

BIRD FEET

The legs were long and thin. Its feet had four toes—three pointed forward and one pointed backward.

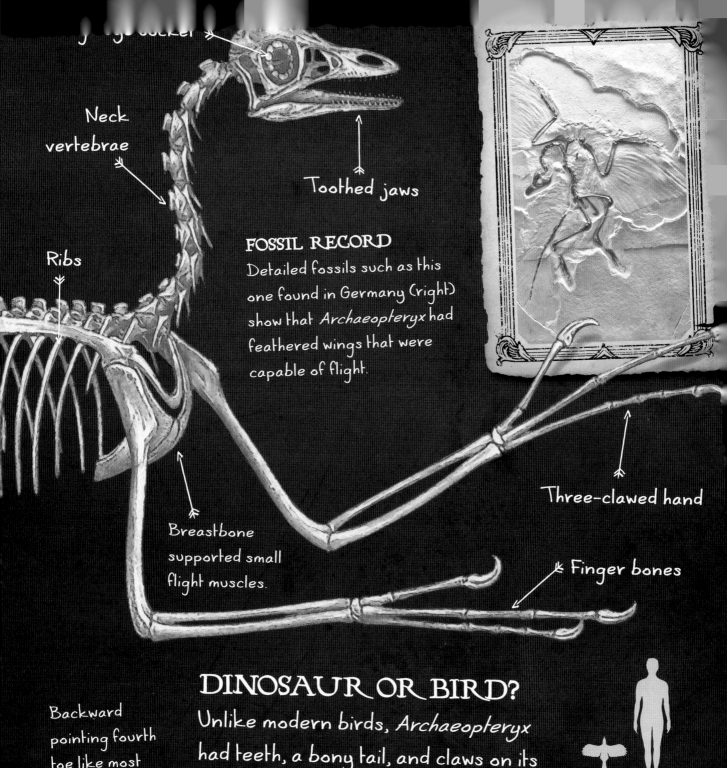

Tongue bucket

Neck
vertebrae

Ribs

Toothed jaws

FOSSIL RECORD
Detailed fossils such as this
one found in Germany (right)
show that *Archaeopteryx* had
feathered wings that were
capable of flight.

Breastbone
supported small
flight muscles.

Three-clawed hand

Finger bones

Backward
pointing fourth
toe like most
modern birds.

DINOSAUR OR BIRD?
Unlike modern birds, *Archaeopteryx*
had teeth, a bony tail, and claws on its
wings. It shared these features with the
dinosaurs of its time. The skeletons
of small feathered animals of this kind
show that birds are living descendants
of the theropod dinosaurs.

Archaeopteryx
was about
14 inches
long—the same

PTEROSAURS

THE pterosaurs were the first large animals to take to the air. Previously, only small animals such as insects could fly. Pterosaurs dominated the air for more than 100 million years before dying out with the dinosaurs.

INSECT EATER
Dimorphodon (left) could snap its short beak shut very quickly. It probably used its swift bite to catch insects.

Quetzalcoatlus

The biggest pterosaur was Quetzalcoatlus. It had a wingspan of 36 feet—that's three times the size of the wandering albatross, the largest bird today. This pterodactyloid lived 67 million years ago in North America.

Short tail

Hand bone

CRESTED PTEROSAUR

Tupuxuara lived between 125 and 115 million years ago in South America. This large pterosaur had a flat, rounded crest on the top of its head. The crest was filled with blood vessels, and may have been brightly colored.

Crest may have changed color to signal to members of the opposite sex.

Tupuxuara had a sharp beak that was probably used to catch fish.

Long neck to dip beak into the water while fishing.

Toothless mouth

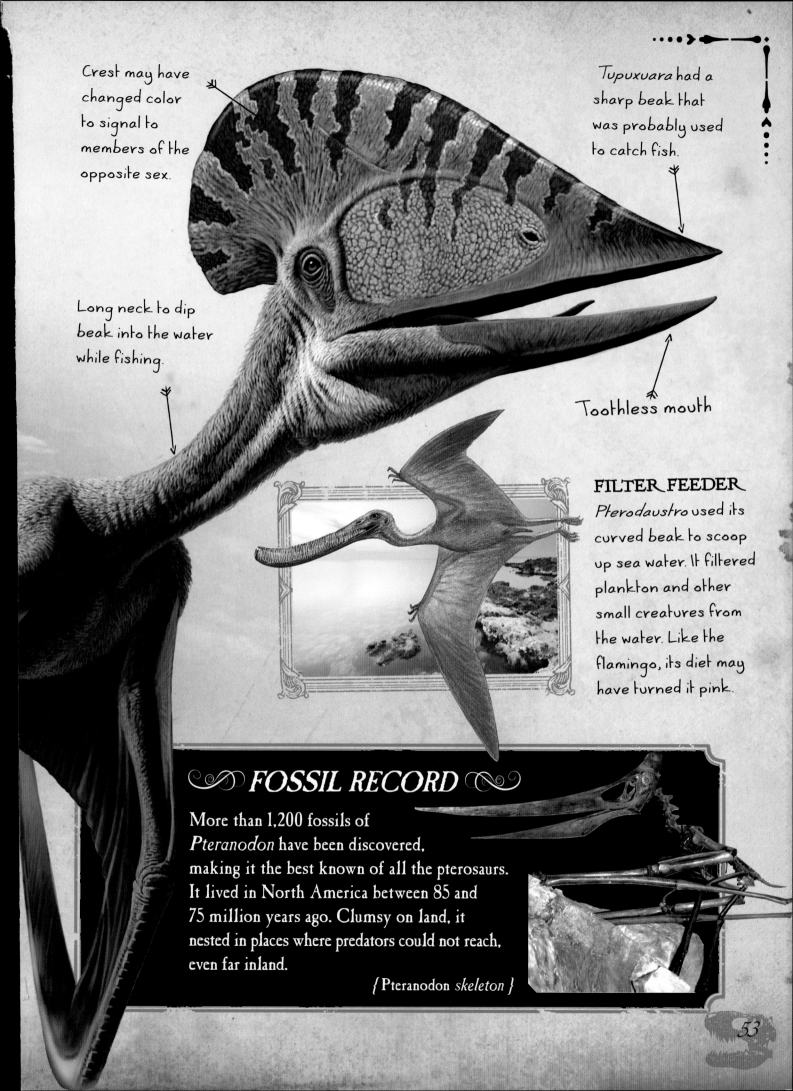

FILTER FEEDER
Pterodaustro used its curved beak to scoop up sea water. It filtered plankton and other small creatures from the water. Like the flamingo, its diet may have turned it pink.

❧ FOSSIL RECORD ❧

More than 1,200 fossils of *Pteranodon* have been discovered, making it the best known of all the pterosaurs. It lived in North America between 85 and 75 million years ago. Clumsy on land, it nested in places where predators could not reach, even far inland.

{ Pteranodon skeleton }

53

ANHANGUERA

Anhanguera's long head was twice the length of its body.

Needlelike teeth

Lower beak crest

Eye socket

Short tail

A bone on the wrist helped to control the wings.

WHEN dinosaurs roamed the land, flying reptiles called pterosaurs ruled the skies. *Anhanguera* was a kind of pterosaur called a pterodactyloid. Its wings were made from skin that was fixed to long finger bones.

DIVING FOR FISH

An expert fish-catcher, *Anhanguera* used its needlelike teeth to grasp hold of its slippery prey. Crests on both its upper and lower beak helped to keep the head steady as it entered the water.

Long fourth finger supported the top edge of the wing.

Anhanguera had a wingspan of 15 feet, but its body was just 8 inches long.

Fingers

Light Bones

Like birds, pterosaurs had to be as light as possible in order to fly. Their bones were thin, and many were hollow to make them even lighter.

Leg bones

Leathery skin was stretched between the fingers and the body to form the wings.

Weak legs suggest that this pterosaur spent most of its time in the air.

Toe bones

Legs and feet were held out behind Anhanguera as it flew.

The first three fingers were short and had sharp claws.

CRAWLER

Anhanguera was probably slow and clumsy on land. It may have crawled on all fours, pulling itself along with the claws on its wings.

There were five toes on each foot. The first four toes had claws.

WATER REPTILES

THE plesiosaurs and their relatives, the fishlike ichthyosaurs, were marine reptiles that evolved from land reptiles. It is unlikely that any of these large creatures ever came ashore.

PLIOSAURS

The giant pliosaurs were the tigers of the Jurassic oceans. They had powerful jaws and sharp teeth and would prey on sharks, ichthyosaurs, and even smaller plesiosaurs. They had large heads and short necks and were built for speed.

LIVE YOUNG

It was once thought that plesiosaurs dragged themselves ashore to lay eggs, but their limbs could not have supported their weight on land. However, a specimen was found with an embryo in the body cavity, which shows that they gave birth to live young in the water.

The rear flippers were larger than the front ones.

FILTER FEEDER

Cryptoclidus (left) had a jaw full of curved teeth. It fed by gulping water and using its teeth as a sieve. These allowed the water to drain out but left food such as shrimp in its mouth.

Kronosaurus

FLIPPERS

To turn the limbs into flippers rather than legs, plesiosaur bones had to change. The bones became flatter, and the elbow and knee joints became fixed.

{ Flipper bones }

FLIPPER BONES

Pliosaur flippers were full of bones. They had five "fingers," and the two long digits in the middle were made of up to 10 bones each.

DEEP DIVER

The whalelike _Liopleurodon_ (above) was a strong swimmer that would dive to great depths to hunt large squid, as sperm whales do today.

Giant Predator

One of the largest pliosaurs of all was _Kronosaurus_. Its skull was nine feet long, and its bite was even more powerful than that of _Tyrannosaurus_.

PLESIOSAURUS

ONE of the earliest of the plesiosaurs, *Plesiosaurus* lived around 185 million years ago. It was not a fast swimmer but could control its movements very precisely with its large flippers, using its long neck to catch fast-swimming fish.

Sharp teeth

Lower jaw

Long, strong neck

BELLY BONES
Belly ribs joined the shoulder and hipbones to make *Plesiosaurus's* short body rigid and strong.

Searching for Prey

Plesiosaurus fed on small to medium-sized fish and squid. It could use its long neck to raise its head high above the water to search for potential prey.

STRONG MUSCLES

The shoulder and hipbones were large and flat. Powerful muscles were attached to the bones to power the flippers.

Plesiosaurus grew up to 11 feet long.

Long backbone

Flat hipbone

Some scientists think the tail may have had a fin to help the animal steer.

Short tail

Belly ribs

Long flippers

BEATING FLIPPERS

Plesiosaurs swam by beating their flippers up and down through the water, like turtles do today. They used their long necks as a rudder to change direction.

STRONG BONES

Each digit contained up to nine bones, giving the flippers strength and flexibility.

OPHTHALMOSAURUS

THE ichthyosaur *Ophthalmosaurus* lived about 160 million years ago. This fishlike reptile spent its whole life at sea, even giving birth in the water. Its body was shaped like a teardrop, and it could swim at up to 25 mph. It used its huge eyes to hunt in deep, dark water.

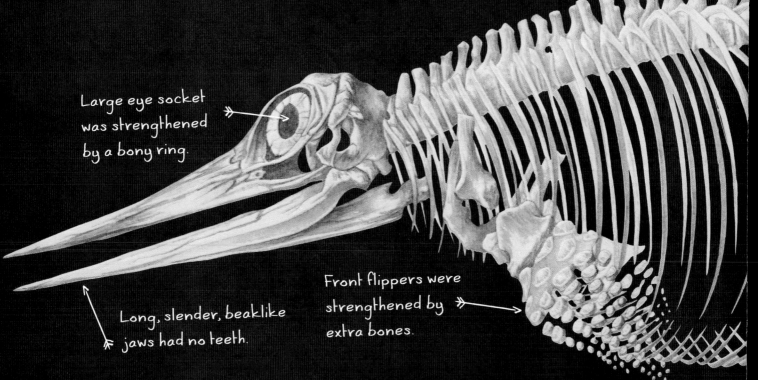

Large eye socket was strengthened by a bony ring.

Long, slender, beaklike jaws had no teeth.

Front flippers were strengthened by extra bones.

Ophthalmosaurus was 12 feet long and weighed nearly one ton.

BREATHING AIR

Ichthyosaurs, like turtles and crocodiles today, had to come to the surface regularly to breathe. *Ophthalmosaurus's* nostrils were at the top of its head, which allowed it to breathe without poking its whole head out of the water.

FISH DIET

Ophthalmosaurus fed on fish, squid, and squidlike belemites. It caught its prey in its toothless beak and swallowed it whole.

TAIL-POWERED

Ophthalmosaurus pushed itself forward with sideways movements of its powerful tail, which had a broad half-moon-shaped fin. It used its strong front flippers to steer.

Rib cage

Strong, flexible backbone

End of tail bone pointed sharply down to support the tail fin.

Rear flippers were small and weak.

Dorsal fin

Born Swimmers

Unlike most reptiles, ichthyosaurs did not lay eggs. Instead, they gave birth in the water to live young. The newborn *Ophthalmosaurus* had to be sufficiently well developed to swim right away.

Babies were born tail-first.

GLOSSARY

AMBUSH HUNTER
Predator that hides and waits for its prey to come close before pouncing.

AMPHIBIAN
Four-limbed vertebrate animal whose reproduction involves the fertilization of eggs laid in water.

CAMBRIAN
Geological period between 541 and 485 million years ago, in which complex animals became widespread in the oceans for the first time.

CARBONIFEROUS
Geological period between 359 and 299 million years ago, in which there was rich plant life in many parts of the world.

CRETACEOUS
Geological period between 145 and 66 million years ago. Many dinosaurs lived in this period, which also saw the evolution of birds and mammals.

DINOSAUR
Group of land reptiles that appeared 230 million years ago and became extinct at the end of the Cretaceous. The dinosaurs included the largest animals ever to walk on land, the sauropods.

EVOLVE
Change in form from an ancestor by a process of gradual changes over generations. New species evolve that are well adapted to survive and reproduce in their environment.

EXTINCT
Description of a species of animal or plant that has completely died out. Mass extinctions of many different species can take place when the environment changes suddenly, such as with climate change.

FOSSIL
Body part, footprint, or other remains of a dead plant, insect, or animal from long ago that has turned to stone, deep within the earth.

ICHTHYOSAUR
Group of large marine reptiles that swam using their tails. They did not lay eggs but gave birth in the water to live young.

JURASSIC
Geological period between 201 and 145 million years ago, during which large dinosaurs dominated the land.

MAMMAL
Warm-blooded animals that usually have hairy bodies. Female mammals produce milk from special glands and use it to feed their young.

METEORITE
Lump of rock that hits Earth from space.

PANGAEA
Giant continent that formed about 240 million years ago and included all the world's land. It started to break up during the Triassic and Jurassic periods.

PELVIS
Bony structure that connects the spine
to the hind legs.

PERMIAN
Geological period between 299 and 252 million
years ago. During this period, Pangaea formed,
and much of the Carboniferous forest was
replaced by deserts.

PLESIOSAUR
Group of large marine reptiles that used flippers
to swim. Unlike the turtles today, plesiosaurs
gave birth to live young at sea.

PREDATOR
Animal that hunts and kills other animals for food.

PREY
Animal that is hunted by a predator.

PTEROSAUR
Group of flying reptiles. Pterosaurs' wings
were made of a thin membrane of skin, like
the wings of bats.

REPTILE
Group of animals that have scaly skin
and mostly lay eggs covered by a shell or
membrane. Dinosaurs, ichthyosaurs, and
pterosaurs were all reptiles. Modern-day
reptiles include crocodiles and lizards.

SCAVENGER
Animal that feeds on the remains of animals
that have died naturally or have been killed
by predators.

SPECIES
Group of living things of the same type. Members
of the same species are very similar to one
another and can breed and produce fertile
offspring.

SYNAPSID
Group of animals that includes mammals and their
reptile ancestors that dominated the land in the
Permian period.

THEROPOD
Group of saurischian dinosaurs that were
primarily meat-eaters. Today's birds evolved
from theropod dinosaurs.

VERTEBRATE
Animal with a backbone that is made up of
a row of bones called vertebrae.

INDEX

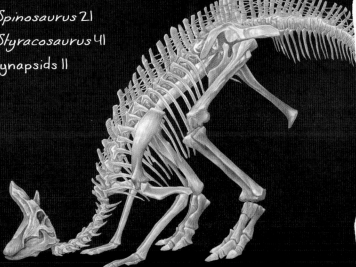

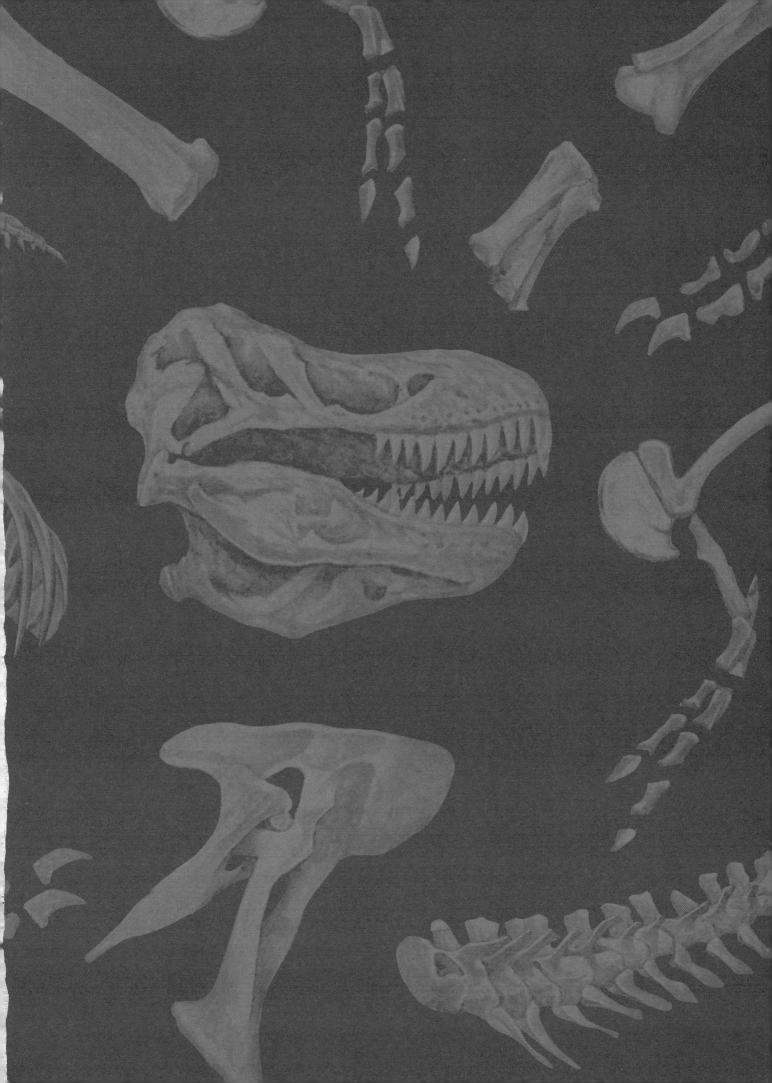

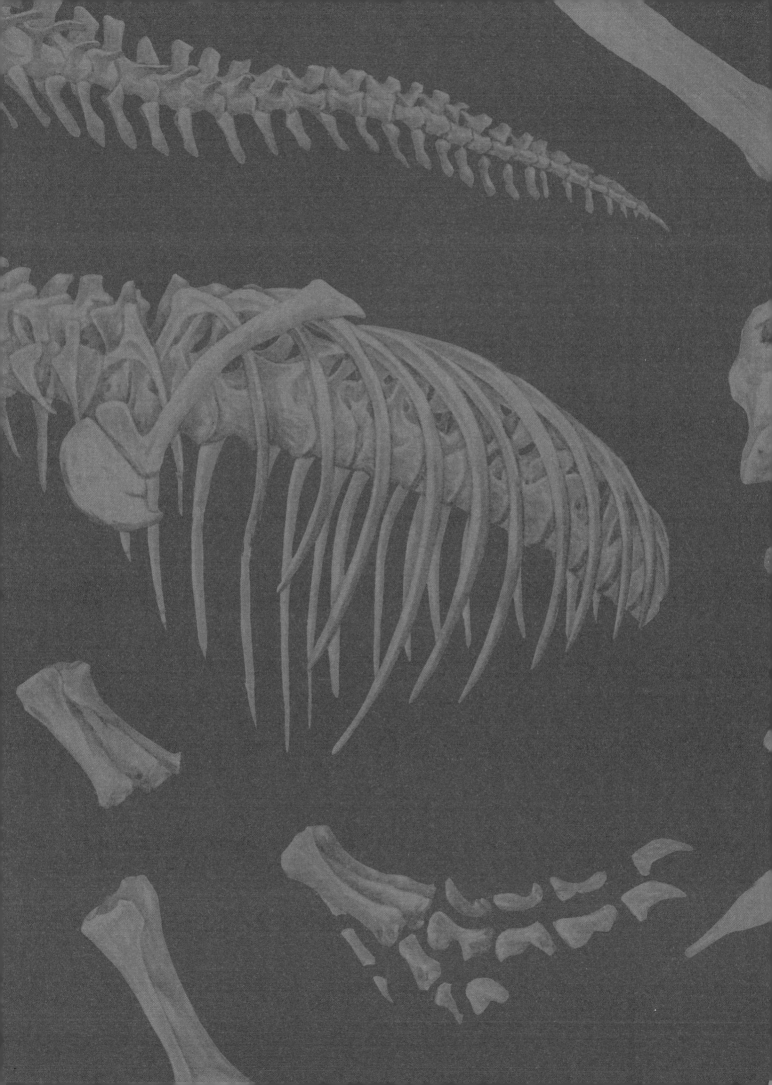

BUILD THE TYRANNOSAURUS REX

CAREFULLY follow the steps below to create your Tyrannosaurus rex skeleton.

{ Align the slots }

JOINING PIECES
The pieces join together slot-to-slot. No glue is needed.

1.

Take the hip (part 1) and slot the body joining strip (4) into the middle slots. **Slot** the front into the hip first and then rotate the back into its slot.

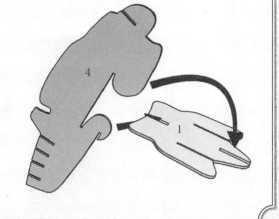

2.

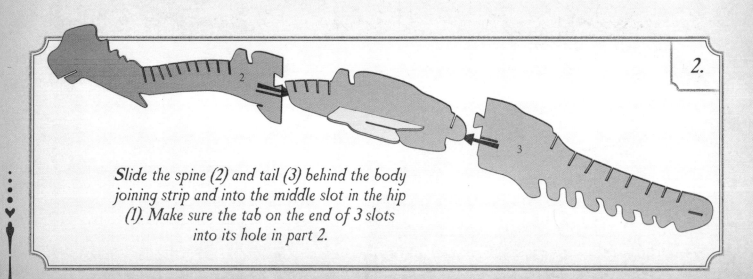

Slide the spine (2) and tail (3) behind the body joining strip and into the middle slot in the hip (1). Make sure the tab on the end of 3 slots into its hole in part 2.

3.

*S*lot the ribs (5–14) and vertebrae (15–22) into the spine and tail.

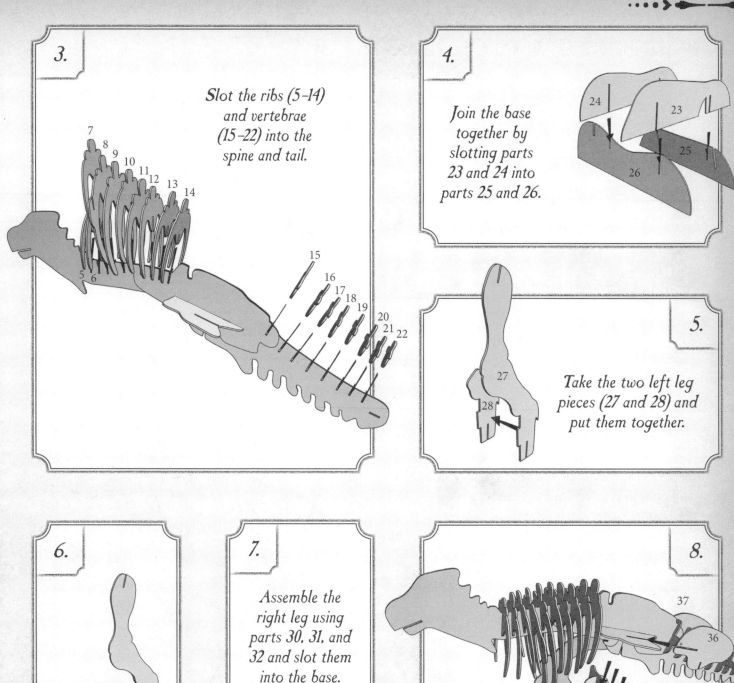

7 8 9 10 11 12 13 14
5 6
15 16 17 18 19 20 21 22

4.

*J*oin the base together by slotting parts 23 and 24 into parts 25 and 26.

24 23 25 26

5.

*T*ake the two left leg pieces (27 and 28) and put them together.

27 28

6.

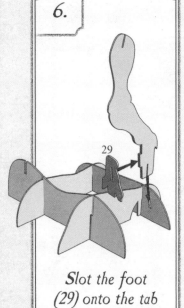

29

*S*lot the foot (29) onto the tab on the bottom of the two joined leg pieces and then slot the leg into the base.

7.

*A*ssemble the right leg using parts 30, 31, and 32 and slot them into the base. *S*lot the two pelvis sides (33 and 34) into the second part of the hip (35).

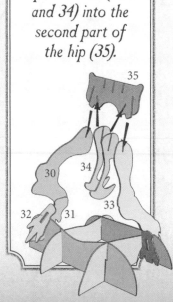

35 34 33 30 32 31

8.

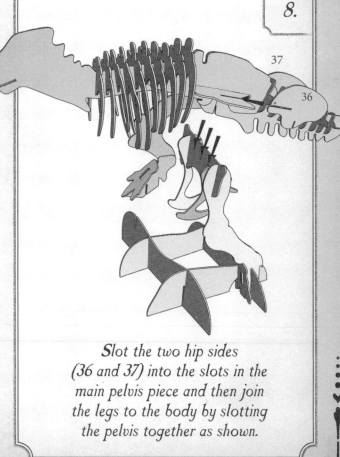

37 36

*S*lot the two hip sides (36 and 37) into the slots in the main pelvis piece and then join the legs to the body by slotting the pelvis together as shown.